INVISIBLE

ALSO BY HUGUES DE MONTALEMBERT

Eclipse

INVISIBLE

A MEMOIR

HUGUES DE MONTALEMBERT

ATRIA BOOKS

NEW YORK   LONDON   TORONTO   SYDNEY

ATRIA BOOKS

A Division of Simon & Schuster, Inc.
1230 Avenue of the Americas
New York, NY 10020

First Atria Books hardcover edition January 2010

ATRIA BOOKS and colophon are trademarks of Simon & Schuster, Inc.

For information about special discounts for bulk purchases, please contact Simon & Schuster Special Sales at 1-866-506-1949 or business@simonandschuster.com.

The Simon & Schuster Speakers Bureau can bring authors to your live event. For more information or to book an event contact the Simon & Schuster Speakers Bureau at 1-866-248-3049 or visit our website at www.simonspeakers.com.

Designed by Dana Sloan

Manufactured in the United States of America

10   9   8   7   6   5   4   3   2   1

Library of Congress Cataloging-in-Publication Data

Montalembert, Hugues de.
    Invisible : a memoir / Hugues de Montalembert.—1st Atria Books hardcover ed.
        p. cm.
1. Montalembert, Hugues de. 2. Montalembert, Hugues de—Travel. 3. Victims of crimes—New York (State)—New York—Biography. 4. Blind—New York (State)—New York—Biography. 5. Blindness—Psychological aspects—Case studies. 6. Life change events—Case studies. 7. French—New York (State)—New York—Biography. 8. New York (N.Y.)—Biography. 9. Painters—France—Biography. 10. Motion picture producers and directors—France—Biography. I. Title.

    HV6250.3.U53N484 2010
    362.88092—dc22
    [B]

                                                                2009041715

    ISBN 978-1-4165-9366-9
    ISBN 978-1-4391-0068-4 (ebook)

To Lin

INVISIBLE

YOU LIVE in a city like New York.

You read the papers.

You look at television.

But you never think it will happen to you.

It happened to me one evening.

Going back to my house near Washington Square I was attacked by, I suppose, people looking for money to buy drugs.

When they saw there was no money in the house, it became quite nasty.

It was no longer for money; it was for, I would say, fun.

There were two of them. A very big one and a smaller, less strong one.

I attacked the big one with a poker; there was a fireplace so I attacked him with a poker.

I could feel he was dangerous. He had a knife.

I didn't pay attention to the little one.

The little one had a weapon in his pocket.

Paint remover.

It's not an acid, it's a base.

If you wash a base with water it doesn't go away.

It continues to dig.

While I was fighting with the big one, the little one threw that paint remover in my face.

I understood that something quite serious had happened.

I thought they would kill me so I started to scream.

I was screaming so loudly that they got scared and they left.

I immediately went to the shower.

But I could see my sight going away, away, away.

I called a friend because I didn't know the telephone number of the police.

I said, Please ask the police to come, I have been attacked.

But I could hardly even see the numbers to dial.

It was already getting difficult.

The police came maybe thirty minutes later.

I was brought to the emergency room of the nearby hospital.

They tried to wash it out, but as it was a base there was nothing to be done.

I could see that I was losing more and more of my sight.

I asked the doctor: Tell me the truth, is it serious?

He said, It's very serious.

I understood that probably I'd lost my sight.

THE MORNING came and already I knew that I was on the way to an irrevocable fate.

By the morning I was totally blind.

So it took me a night; it was very fast, very drastic.

And then you find yourself lying in a bed with that new situation at hand.

With that new person.

You are somebody who used to be totally free and could look and see.

I was a painter and I was making films.

My life was based on seeing.

IT WAS not total darkness, I could see a light.

Even if my eyelids were closed, I could still see through my eyelids.

I could see a golden light.

I was not in total darkness for another reason, which at first was incredibly disturbing.

My brain, wanting to see images but not receiving any perceptions through the eyes, would create very strong images on its own.

Vivid images.

It got to the point where I would be talking to you and suddenly I would see something like a vision, totally produced by the brain, absolutely real to me.

Very strong images, very disturbing.

For example, I would see the head of a man in marble. Just a head and two white globes, his eyes, globes in white marble. And suddenly I would see black lightning on them, as if those two white globes would crumble in cracks of black light.

I see the cracks of my own retina. My brain can see those cracks and creates an image with it.

OTHER TIMES I would see very strong, erotic images. Sometimes talking with somebody it was rather disturbing, because suddenly those very strong, erotic images would appear.

Very beautiful, but disturbing.

And I wondered: Why erotic?

I think when a human being is in touch with death—and I have been in touch with death because I really thought I would be killed, and of course I spent three months lying in bed, which is not life—the body has a very strong animal reaction. A very strong sexual drive, if the person doesn't fall into a nervous breakdown.

If he still or she still has appetite for life, sexual desire drives away the sense of danger and the fear of death.

It's not that you run after the nurses exactly, but you try to have an erotic communication with them.

Not all the nurses, but if there is someone you connect with, yes, you will establish something or you will take advantage of that, and you may end up having a rather polygamous life. You become very sexually active just to fight death, if you have a strong instinct for life.

It is very strange because women are sensitive to it and they feel it.

I suppose you sense eroticism.

After that, of course you take confidence in life itself. You establish a new life and you don't need the erotic connection so much.

But that reaction, I would say, is perfectly normal. And I would wish it for anybody who experiences blindness or any other rupture, physical or moral, in his life, to go into that survival instinct. I am sure conventional morality, churches or whatever, will not advocate it, but I think it's a good thing to do.

Looking back at those times of my life, I believe I have been saved, mentally saved from nervous breakdown and despair, by women.

Because they know how to handle life, they know how to give birth. After my blindness, I was in the situation of someone who had to give birth to himself.

I am between death and birth. Dead to my past life and not yet reborn to this new one. This whole period is merely an extraordinary labor through which I am giving birth to myself.

MEN STOOD awkwardly with their feet inward, a bit embarrassed, not knowing how to handle the situation. It
was difficult to have relations with my male friends. It was
much easier with women. They were less embarrassed.

I am finished, finished.

In the hospital, I grope for the bell. Nine minutes go by, then a dragging footstep.

—Yes!

—I'm in pain; give me a shot.

—We can't give you that regularly. You'd become addicted.

Or sometimes they give it to me without any discussion. Then everything relaxes, I feel good, I am warm, my limbs stretch out, the tension leaves my neck. I will have all the courage I need. I smile; I wish someone were here so we could enjoy a good talk. The drug flows smoothly in my veins, with tenderness, and I abandon myself without remorse, without fear. Take a rest from this nightmare from which you cannot escape. Music in my headphones takes charge of my body and carries it into a world of sensations without landscape.

If they refuse to give me a shot, I say nothing, out of

pride and because I'm curious to see just how deep I'm going to sink. I listen to the noises of the abyss; I expect at any time the intrusion of cold, blind monsters. I sink. The pressure rises. My lungs no longer swell. Blackness is total, liquid, and palpable. It enters through my nose, my ears, my mouth. Night is going to collapse. What is the point of this battle for hope?

WHEN I WAS creating those images, after a while, my brain would get completely tired and like a computer, would shut off—shut off from life.

It was as if my inner eyelids had been torn out. There was nothing to interrupt this exhausting face-to-face confrontation within myself.

Interned within myself, internal imprisonment, submitting to the temptation of the invisible.

Every morning, I leave my dreams, the only moments during which my sight is restored, and again I face the disappointment of reality.

EACH MORNING I believed it wasn't going to happen.

But it did and suddenly by 10:30 I was sucked down by it, left in darkness.

Each morning for three hours, I could have a normal conversation.

After that I couldn't communicate with anybody.

I was left in darkness and paralyzed.

If you are in the dark and you don't know how to move, you are paralyzed.

I was lying on a bed unable to function; I couldn't take that amount of darkness.

It was like falling into a pot of dark honey.

Blindness is a monster. Not physical blindness, which is a mere mechanical accident that prevents images from reaching the brain, but the psychic blindness brought about by that privation. This beast had to be tamed every morning, pitilessly, as soon as I woke up, so that it wouldn't invade my day. A fight not to be the prey of darkness, to re-create light, life. Sometime I felt so cold, so tired, in such danger.

Every morning I wake up full of energy, optimism, and appetite for the day that is about to begin; every evening there is the feeling of defeat. Day after day I am defeated.

WHEN I FINALLY understood what was going on, I said: Let's do like animals: wait, sleep, and don't despair.

If you observe animals—I was born in the country-side—when they are wounded they don't make a fuss. They go into a corner and they sleep and they wait to heal.

"Sleep, wait, and don't think and don't despair. It will change."

Thank God it has changed. It would have been terrible if not.

I don't want to bother with my eyes any longer. I don't want anyone to talk to me about them. I let others be responsible for treating them with balm. I don't want to go on being the gardener of these dead flowers. The others see only the closed petals, but I know very well that the pistil is dead.

Two fingers on my shoulder and the voice of Dr. T.:

—I have to talk to you.

I am surprised at the warm intensity he communicates to me by the pressure of his fingers, even though his voice remains cold. This finger language has been established between us over the course of the past days.

He pushes my wheelchair to his office.

I already know that something is wrong. The animal in me can smell it. His monotonous voice informs me:

—Your eyes are not doing well. The tissues are dis-

solving and I fear perforation. I must perform an abla-
tion of the left eye.

*What a blow! I feel nauseous. Without understand-
ing its complete meaning, I know that this sentence an-
nounces something horrible.*

I STAYED three months in the hospital because we tried everything.

I had three operations and not one was a success.

So, three months later, I found myself out in the street holding the arm of somebody and totally scared of the outside world, of the street, of the noise, of everything.

I am released from the hospital with six stitches in each eye, blind, handicapped, feeling nausea for life, for lifetime. I do not say this to paint a gloomy picture; I am trying to explain, as best I can, the fear and mental anguish of those who, like me, have been stabbed in the heart of life.

Out of the door of the hospital, my legs feel like cotton and I am already exhausted. The noise of the city swallows me. The cars seem to be heading right for me. Impossible to get my bearings in this neighborhood even though I know it by heart down to the smallest detail: Greenwich Avenue, Eleventh Street, Christopher Street. Geometrical lines and the points of the compass danced in my head.

I will never be able to function again.

INDEPENDENCE IS essential—to be able to master your own life. To be dependent, not to be the captain aboard my own ship, that is where my handicap lives. My independence is in a cage.

"Will I go back to life? Will I be captain again?"

If you can go back to life, if you can keep on being the captain on board, then life is fantastic, then life is an adventure, your own and unique adventure. You dance with life, you dance with the Universe.

"Go back to life!" At the beginning, you think it's impossible.

You go in the street for the first time, you see nothing, you hear chaos, and nothing is structured. Into chaos you cannot move. You have to recreate the World, you have to organize the chaos. I tell you, forget the Bible, it takes more than seven days to create a world.

• • •

I suppose you become like a computer receiving, without being aware, billions of tiny, tiny little bits of information.

And at the end your brain builds a visual image.

At first not very precise, hazy. And then it becomes so clear.

And that's why probably it was not so difficult for me to adapt to the situation of not seeing; my brain was so visually trained. Automatically it was producing images all the time.

Images exactly like a film.

I was making films in my head.

When I became blind, I didn't stop seeing, I just had to do all that work myself so I was exhausted . . . so exhausted. But little by little it became less exhausting.

WHEN I WAS on the hospital bed, I said to myself: How many blind people have you met in the thirty-five years of your life?

I met one, a formidable guy in Indonesia, who had populated alone, by himself, with his balls, an island on the coast of Sumbawa where I stayed a month or more. Quite an extraordinary guy who had become blind when he was around sixty.

I met another one in Benin, he was a kind of voodoo priest who could speak with birds and so I filmed him. Those were not even intimate meetings.

I never met blind people socially.

So I thought: Where are they?

There is a pit somewhere, where, nicely, with the help of society, they are dumped.

I don't want to go there.

WHEN IT happened to me, when I was attacked and found myself in the hospital, I said, First of all don't say anything to my family, to my girlfriend or, you know, anybody too close to me.

Because I have to deal with it alone, otherwise I will have to console my family or my girlfriend and so on.

Give me some days or weeks to deal with it first.

And then of course my family was informed.

People called them behind my back.

My mother said that she would come to New York. And I said—please, don't.

That would have been a lot of trouble for me because I would have found my mother in tears and had to console her, and so on.

Who wants to be a source of sorrow for someone he loves? It is not my mission to be a redeemer and so I have no good reason to plunge a dagger into my mother's heart, like the images of the Virgin in the village church.

I said, I'm perfectly all right, don't worry.

With enough protection from society, protection from family, you will find yourself in that marvelous pit I was talking about.

REAL BLINDNESS is fear.

If you don't dive into the action and stay alive and awake and aware and enjoy your life with a free mind, it is due to fear.

Fear of life is the first enemy of the blind.

To avoid falling in the pit, I forced myself to behave naturally and not blindly.

I am frightened of being frightening.

I have to understand who I am for others.

YOU HAVE to walk and present yourself not as a blind person but as a normal human being.

Very often, especially with those who are born blind, but even with those blinded by accident or illness, they don't look at the person to whom they are speaking. You look at the person with your ears, because you cannot see and read lips as everybody else does.

If I position my head in a certain way, I can see your lips with my ears. You will see many blind people walking or talking with their heads looking up or looking down.

Instead of having such behavior, there is a normal way to present oneself, which is to look straight at the other person. It may seem superficial, but really it is very important, because by correcting it, you will have a normal relationship with the person with whom you are trying to communicate.

Strangely enough, this behavior is not taught in rehabilitation centers.

I WAS amazed by the number of people who would come into my hospital room, people I didn't know, from the staff, nurses, doctors, or patients. They would sit and they would tell me the most intimate details of their lives.

I became a bit disturbed by that phenomenon.

I confided my feelings to a doctor. He laughed and said:

"Why do you think Dr. Freud was sitting *behind* the sofa?"

The fact that they cannot be seen is liberating for many people.

In the Catholic church they have those little boxes where you make your confession and it is very dark and you can't see the priest and you hope he can't see you. And so you feel free to confess your sins.

For the same reason, many couples talk in the car because then they don't have to make eye contact.

Late at night, thanks to my insomnia, I discover radio programs of a special kind. Just a studio with open telephone lines. Sometimes the broadcast has a theme, and all around there are people listening in New York City and the entire metropolitan area, New Jersey, and Connecticut. Anyone who wants to can call in. Everything is anonymous; people can make their confessions without being identified. One night the theme is cruising. In answer to the question "What is your best asset?" the women as well as the men respond: "Eyes." Meeting eyes. So, solitude is broken through the eyes.

IF YOU love somebody and you cannot look into the eyes of the person, something is missing.

All the rest, her beauty, the shape of her body, you see everything, but—the expression in her eyes, that is something you will never be able to touch.

For some people it is unbearable. For love, not to see or not to be seen, can be unbearable.

How many times have you walked in the street or been in the subway and you just make eye contact with somebody and something happens?

And maybe it will even change your life.

I met a woman in Denmark.

She was riding a little train between Elsinore and Copenhagen.

A man sat opposite her, just looking at her, and after ten minutes he said, "I love you; you are the woman of my life."

And they have been married now for fifteen years, completely happy.

I LOST many friends along with my sight.

My girlfriend at that time refused to see me.

Some people can't cope with it—that's all.

But I didn't think much of it at the time.

I was too much absorbed in my own fight to go back to life to take care of that. It didn't depress me; I was too busy elsewhere.

I had a very good friend who couldn't come to the hospital. He said: I will see you—but after, when you have left the hospital.

People don't like tragedy.

A doctor comes to see me regularly. He's a cancer specialist; he refuses to sit down and says nothing. I feel myself being observed, which makes me uncomfortable. Today he broke his silence to say:

—I would hate for my life to be a tragedy, because, after all, I have only one.

—So would I, *echoes a nurse.*

I keep silent, for they are right. But it is my life and even if I'm blind, I love my life.

WHAT I LEARNED very soon was not to present myself in any way as a tragic figure; otherwise you will be isolated.

THE DOCTORS told me that I would have a nervous breakdown.

The nervous breakdown never came.

And I said, What about that rehabilitation center?

They said, It's much too soon.

I felt it was not too soon at all, that if I waited longer I would get depressed by rotting in some corner.

My body feels inconsistent, my joints stiff. "Put a stop to this deterioration, phone the rehabilitation center."

—Hello. Lighthouse. Good afternoon!

I explain, I request; they switch me from one department to another.

—We'll send someone in a few days to evaluate you.

WHEN I FACED my first night alone, I stood with my feet deep in the carpet for a long time without moving, leaning my forehead against the wall, listening to the mounting panic. Panic against which the force of all my will could only erect a fragile barrier. I felt that the slightest movement of my body could break the dike and that this thing which I didn't even want to define would surge up in me like thirty thousand galloping barbarians, leaving me devastated. I heard the sounds of my body, the way I swallow, the circulation of life. Then, little by little, the sounds of the city through the window, the sirens at a nearby hospital, all that New York violence which used to fascinate me, like being given permission to visit hell.

What meaning was I to find in what had happened to me? This question obsessed me. If there is no meaning in it, then it is terrible, because there is no worse punishment. Such agony, a twenty-four-hour-a-day struggle to overcome fear. My courage puzzles me but it is not mine; it is the courage of this living species, the human being.

There is a force in me that does not belong to me but that is everybody's; in the same way my weakness, my neuroses, and my weariness do not belong to me, nor does my despair, which is never very far off. Sometimes, I don't even know if I am pretending to be what I am or if that is what I really am.

Three days later, Mrs. Finklestein, an instructor in mobil-
ity and orientation, rings my doorbell. She has brought
a folding cane, and we go down to the street.

—Try to walk on your own.

The fracas of the two-way traffic on Eighty-sixth
Street makes my head swim and I instinctively walk to-
ward the buildings to escape danger. "Good Lord, how
can anyone walk alone without being able to see?" I'm
afraid.

—Take my arm.

We walk. I hear the row of buildings come to an
end. My head is struck so brutally by the sun that I float
in the light. We have just left the shadow of Eighty-sixth
Street. I have completely lost my sense of direction.
Through my stitched eyelids, I see. It may not be much,
but when I see the shadow of my hand between the sun
and myself, I experience equally the pleasure and the
absurdity of the situation. I feel that between the world

and me there is nothing more than a thin leaf of ciga-rette paper and that it would take very little to tear it.

I listen to the vast canyon of Madison Avenue.

—Where are we? *she asks me as a test.*

—On the northeast corner of Madison and Eighty-sixth.

—No. We're on the southwest corner of Park Avenue and Eighty-sixth.

I don't understand and think back over the way we came. I had simply assumed that my apartment build-ing was on the north side of the street, but it's on the south side. It will take several weeks to erase this mis-take from my brain. In fact I think I never got rid of it completely. And that's how I became aware of some-thing that will happen often. When it comes to orienta-tions, every clue is printed in indelible characters on my memory. This is an advantage in that I am able to reg-ister a place, a house, an apartment, an itinerary once and for all. I can return much later and find my direction without thinking. On the other hand, if I absentmindedly make a mistake, I go on repeating the same mistake endlessly.

—What hints might have helped you realize you were wrong?

It's like a game; I feel my brain get stimulated.

—I hear that this avenue is much larger than Madison and that there is traffic in both directions, while Madison is one-way.

—Could you tell me what color the traffic lights are?

Easy! I listen carefully. The stream of cars flows in front of me and comes to a stop, then the cars on my left start up and go east on Eighty-sixth Street.

—Red light on Park Avenue, green on Eighty-sixth Street.

We wait for the lights to change some more, and I follow them without any trouble.

—That way you will be able to choose the right moment to cross the street. We are going around the block.

—Where are we?

—Northeast corner of Eighty-fifth and Madison.

—Lean on the sound of the traffic line. That is the clue you will have to use to walk straight.

I listen but I don't understand how this chaotic

noise will help me walk straight. Far from being a line, the noise strikes me as being a huge inkblot, and besides, all I want to do now is to go home to the silence of my apartment, to go away from Mrs. Finklestein's professional voice.

—You should be able to learn quickly, *she says.*

SO I FORCED my way into that rehabilitation center.

That was in Manhattan, it was called the Lighthouse.

And for a year and a half, I would say, I worked very, very hard at regaining a little bit of independence.

That was my aim: to become independent.

So I learned how to cook, how to sew a button, everything to be independent.

But mainly to walk alone.

It's education without love. In such a process, love is even discouraged; it could only impede rehabilitation. It's a very tough business.

It's a new life, a sort of reincarnation.

You have to learn everything again like a little child but without the help of your mother. You have to learn to walk and to be independent.

THEY STARTED to teach me how to walk in the building of the rehabilitation center, in the corridors—to take the lift.

You learn pretty fast.

Then they test you to see what ability you have.

I remember there was a corridor. It was a very long, large corridor and they asked me to walk from one end to the other end.

In the middle I stopped and they said, Why did you stop?

—Because there is an obstacle in front of me.

—Yes, what is it?

—I don't know; usually there is no obstacle there.

I could sense that I could maybe go around it on the left and on the right.

I clicked my finger and I said I might go under it.

They said, It's a blackboard that we put on a tripod in the middle of the corridor to see if you would detect it.

So it meant that I had what they called very good facial vision, which is absolutely like a bat's. You receive the waves of the walls or obstacles and, if you have it, you will be able to detect danger and sense obstacles with greater facility.

So I was very happy to know that. I could feel that I was using it instinctively all the time. It develops in time, but at first you either have it or you don't.

I started to learn to walk with a girl who worked for the Lighthouse. She taught me, but it was very slow going.

The process of rehabilitation, which began scarcely two months ago, is slow. In spite of excellent "facial vision," as they call it, which helps me detect obstacles, I'm still practicing on the fifth-floor corridor of the Lighthouse. Lesley, the instructor I've been assigned to, teaches me how to make even arcs with my cane. I advance my right foot, the cane touches the floor to my left, I advance my left foot, the cane traces an arc and touches the floor to my right. Whether or not I progress in a straight line depends on how uniform the arc is.

IT'S ANOTHER reality, it's another dimension.

What you do is you hear the walls of the buildings, you hear if there is a car passing in the street; it gives you parallels and you have to move between those parallels.

It's a very abstract world of sounds mainly. And your feet have to become like hands. I used to wear very thin-soled shoes, sand shoes. I would use really everything. Everything I needed to go back to life, because I understood it was a very difficult job.

So, every day I worked to regain freedom, but all I was aware of was the absence of my life.

And morning after morning, the sun would rise and the radio would announce: "Today, clear visibility." My foot!

Some people find a meaning in what has happened to me.

A teacher of transcendental meditation tells me:

"It is a blessing from God!"

"No! Don't insult God."

I squeeze my cane, which I feel like breaking on his head.

In a lecture at the Lighthouse, someone who lost his sight in an accident declares, "Since I've been blind, I have become a much better person."

"Cut off your legs; you'll be even better!" I shout to him from my seat.

A blind Hindu who recently arrived here from Bombay is the only one who laughs. The others think I have problems. I leave the lecture laughing with Jet, the Hindu.

. . .

One morning, while taking a shower, I drop the soap and, absentmindedly, bend over to pick it up. One of the wall faucets hits my left eye, the more fragile one. Two stitches give way.

The eye is more or less all right but another operation is needed.

In my room at the hospital I find a man who had his brow ridge and nose broken when he was punched right in the face by an unknown passerby.

"I live in New Jersey," he says, "but every year for our wedding anniversary my wife and I go dancing in a club on Sixth Avenue. Oh, no big deal; it's just a little joint that has good music. And can you believe it! We leave the place around midnight and that guy smashes my face in right there outside the club and leaves. Shit! He didn't even stop. And nobody tried to stop him, either."

"Hard luck," I say.

"Not at all. Just the opposite! The three weeks I've spent here have been the best of my life. The nurses have been taking wonderful care of me; they pamper

me and everybody has left me in peace. You see, for thirty-eight years I worked in a bank. Oh, I wasn't a director or executive. No, just an ordinary clerk. Then it was time to retire. The kids were off on their own and I was bored stiff around the house. The fucking house, the fucking dog, and the fucking wife!"

Later in the afternoon, his wife came in to get him. It was his last day at the hospital.

"Hello, hello, darling. How glad you must be to go home at last! If you could see the dog! He is jumping all over the house; he knows you're coming home today. . . ."

The guy says to me, in a whisper, "See what I mean?"

PEOPLE OFTEN think that their individual fate is everything.

How wrong we are!

It is enough to contemplate the invisible to know how much there is that is greater than fate.

Yes, close your eyes, you will see what light renders invisible.

You will see the little shadow in the shadow.

You will see the signature from beyond.

Listen to that fountain; don't you see every tiny drop of water sparkling in the dark?

There is the meaning.

AMONG THE blind there is probably a temptation to believe that their condition automatically puts them on a higher spiritual plane. Very often the people around them encourage it. Sincerely, I refuse to go along with this farce. Priests talk to me and I hear in their voices a kind of complicity that they take for granted, something to do with the suffering of Jesus on the cross, Jesus and me, our shared crucifixion. What an imposture! I don't want to lose contact with my own reality. Loss of sight is a mechanical accident, not a state of grace or an event fraught with spiritual consequences.

Deep down, I suspect that all this has no meaning. The thought grows little by little, and it both soothes and torments me. And then it makes me laugh; meaning is so much beyond our ability to grasp.

But I keep silent, I don't want to be rejected by my tribe. People do not like to be alone. They feel stronger in a group. And I am afraid, like everybody else, of nights out on the steppes, without the shelter of a roof and tender arms.

FOR A personal reason, one day after seven months of that training, I wanted to see somebody in the middle of the night and I said: I'm sure I can walk alone in the street.

I waited until three o'clock in the morning when the city is extremely quiet and you can use all the sounds.

The night is warm; it touches my face, my hands. I stand still for a while, my long fiberglass cane held in front of me like a fencing foil ready for a duel with darkness. Immobile, I create a vacuum inside myself; become a nocturnal animal blending into the night. Sounds of emptiness echo from the neighboring garage, drawing me in. I resist and follow a straight line. There's the bank whose glass walls form the corner of the street where I am staying, Sixty-third, with Madison Avenue.

I cross the avenue, to the west side, which I know better, and calmly begin to walk uptown. When my cane taps against the metal trapdoors that cover cellars under the sidewalk, I instinctively go around to avoid stepping on them. I hate anything that covers a void. At one point, I stop without really knowing why; my brain is flashing the danger signal. I put my hand out slowly and, a foot from my face touch a metal pole that my inexperienced cane had not detected. Yes indeed, good facial vision. A few blocks later, I hear voices, laughter, and a radio playing salsa music. They are coming toward me and sound slightly drunk or stoned. In any case, it's too late to cross the street, and the worst thing would be to show my fear. I force myself to walk at a steady pace and to swing my cane from side to side in even arcs. My nerves are stretched to the breaking point. A few yards from the group I hear the voices stop although the radio goes on. They have seen me. They are silent as I pass by them, then a voice says:

—Hey, man!

I answer:

—Hi! Lovely night.

Another voice says:

—Yes, sir!

But the tension has been so great that I have lost count of the streets. I don't know whether I'm at Seventy-second, Seventy-third, or Seventy-fourth. The only thing to do is cross Madison again, and when I feel the rubber matting of the Hotel Carlyle under my feet I'll know that I'm between Seventy-sixth and Seventy-seventh. I walk faster and faster, with enthusiasm for this newfound freedom. In fact, I am covered with sweat and my hand grips the cane as if trying to graft it onto my palm. I force my fingers to relax and become aware of how much they hurt.

When I reach Ninety-second Street, I search for a phone booth and find one a block farther on. A sleepy voice tells me that she's much better, that she is sleeping, and that she will bring me some croissants in the morning.

This is perfectly all right with me, and anyhow the night is too exciting for me to be the least bit disappointed. You thought the important thing was to go and comfort that woman! You are forgetting what the old sailor Abdul Jemal told you on the Flores Sea: "Of little importance is the port, it's the voyage that counts."

I knew the place, Madison Avenue, I knew it like the palm of my hand, but it's quite different to walk, even down the street you know perfectly well, with your eyes closed.

It went well.

So I understood that I would be able to move independently.

When I told the story to the Lighthouse, they were not pleased; they thought it was much too soon, it was dangerous, but I knew I was getting there.

The excitement of having done that was overwhelming. So excited, so excited, I was laughing and crying inside myself.

YES, I HAD seen the world and, moreover, peered at it with insatiable curiosity. I was a slow traveler. I would spend weeks, sometimes more than a year, without caring to move. My reasons for remaining in one place were often very different. In the Benin, it was because of my friendship with the old king of Abomey. His Majesty King Sagbajou was 103 years old, and 103 years in Africa throws you into the age of mythology. In Vietnam, it was the war that kept me there, with its sinister spectacle. Sometimes I would shoot a documentary film for television; other times, I'd just keep still and write. Anything would do in order to observe those other selves, so alien and yet so familiar. This passionate wandering lasted for a dozen years, until I was mugged and lost my sight for life.

My burning question was: "And now what? Will my playground be reduced to a small apartment and a city block?"

Traveling . . . just the idea of it terrified me. I mean traveling as I had always done, alone and independent.

Finally, I became an excellent traveler around Manhattan. I would make a few mistakes, like one day climbing onto a bus and throwing my cigarette into a woman's purse as she jumped off. She proceeded to walk up Madison Avenue, to everyone's astonishment, with smoke blowing out of her bag.

By coincidence, I find Bandigo again. Bandigo is a bay horse I had ridden a few years earlier in the forest of Shelter Island. Through various sales, he had ended up in upstate New York. I remember him very clearly as being impulsive but not tricky and decide to ride him again. I ask to be left alone in his stall and speak to him very gently, blowing softly into his nostrils so that he can breathe my smell and get to know me. I look him straight in the eyes, hoping he will understand the absence of my sight.

Outside, I jump into the saddle and it is as if it had been yesterday. But as soon as he moves and begins to dance in the brisk cold air, I get vertigo, I have completely lost touch with the ground, I float in space.

Under me this animal brings back a longing for freedom, for galloping, for large open spaces, for everything that I am now denied.

The walls of my prison will not dissolve.

AFTER MORE or less a year and a half of rehabilitation, I boarded a plane and I went to Indonesia alone.

Completely afraid, I mean afraid just to leave my house in New York, I nonetheless gave up the rent and everything and packed the few things I had.

My main fear was to cross the threshold of the door to my house. To close the door, to walk toward something when you have no idea how it will go.

I hadn't told anyone that I was going to Indonesia, because I knew everybody would say, You are completely mad, you have to wait, at least take somebody with you. . . .

So I preferred to say nothing and I went.

It was a pretty tough decision. But it saved me, I suppose, because where I really went was back to life.

Little by little, you learn. You arrive at the airport, you meet somebody, you talk and you discover that in fact there is a dynamic in traveling like that, without seeing, which organizes itself and everything goes perfectly all right, perfectly well. Maybe you will be stuck, well, you wait and something will always happen: a person will walk by, an opportunity will arise.

It's very important for me to be able to travel alone without seeing. Let's say, it's like a cross between a peculiar sport and yoga. It wakes you up. You have to become intensely aware. The first rule is: There is no time. You must abolish time. You can't be too obstinate. If you don't arrive exactly when you wanted to, or where you wanted to, it doesn't matter.

What matters is to not be submissive, not to be negative, not to be beaten no matter what happens, to always find inside yourself the way out.

I ARRIVED in Singapore and I had to change planes. The Chinese passport people, they said, You are traveling alone?

I said yes.

They said, You cannot travel alone. We don't accept blind people traveling alone.

I could have had a very strong reaction to that and gotten mad, and lost my time and my energy.

I heard that there was somebody waiting behind me, ready to present his passport.

I turn around and said, Where are you going?

He said, Jakarta.

I said, You are traveling with me, aren't you?

He said, Yes of course.

So I turned toward the Chinese officer and I said, I am accompanied.

Instead of getting angry, you just have to find the way out at once and smile.

. . .

I am a very impatient person, so it was very good for
my character to do that. I discovered that it works very
well.

AT THE airport in Jakarta, a man sat beside me and asked if I had a light for his cigarette. I know that a man who asks a blind person for a light is probably asking for something else.

"Where are you from?" I asked him.

"I am Australian but I was born in Poland."

"Australian from Poland . . . you mean you are a Jew."

"Yes."

And suddenly I found myself listening to the most astounding story. His story.

At the age of fourteen he was put in the death camp of Birkenau. His duty every morning was to hold the mirror in front of an SS officer while he was shaving. The young boy's only possessions were four American cigarettes. For three days he observed the officer, then he decided to gamble and when the shaving was finished, that day, he handed him one cigarette. It was in 1944, Germany was suffering and Virginian tobacco was rare. The officer looked silently at it and finally took it. He talked to his orderly who left and came back with a sandwich. The following day, the boy did the same thing, gave his second cigarette and again received a sandwich. And this until the fourth and last cigarette. But even after, the sandwich continued to be brought and that's how he survived until the liberation of that camp while famine, typhus, and dysentery were killing prisoners by the thousands.

Suddenly he said, "S'cuse me, they are calling for boarding, good-bye."

A few minutes later, I was myself boarding my flight to Denpasar. In the seat next to mine was nobody else but that exact same man. All the way to Denpasar, we didn't exchange a word. He had unloaded his soul to somebody who couldn't see him. Out of respect, I pretended not to notice him.

So, sometimes you also meet people because your eyes cannot meet.

I WENT to Bali. Years ago I had lived there. I absolutely loved the place. At the time, there was no tourism and practically no electricity, no cars. It was like a fairy-tale country with beautiful people, beautiful music, theater, dance. In a strange way, I wanted to go back to a country that was of such high visual quality. I suppose my brain, without my knowing, was asking for images, hoping to see. The stronger a visual surrounding you find yourself in, the more, maybe, your brain will catch something.

And on top of everything, I was bankrupt, so I decided to write a book.

I had Indonesian friends—I knew how gentle and refined those people are and I could speak Bahasa Indonesia. I stayed one year.

I wrote the book and I thought life was perfectly okay.

To write the book, because I had no electricity in the house for my electric typewriter, I used big notebooks and a piece of cardboard with which I would align my writing, sliding it down every line. It was not so easy to write that way, yet it did work.

I think I wrote something like eight hundred pages by hand.

Sometimes the ink would run out and I would go on writing without knowing there was no ink.

The morning after I used to ask the Balinese working in my house, where did I finish yesterday on the page? And one day, the girl cooking for me, she said, *Tida ada tulis.*

There is no writing.

I said, What do you mean, there is no writing?

No, *tida ada*, there is none.

So we went back—*Tida ada*. For twelve pages there was no writing.

Once you have written something, I discovered you can't write it again. It's gone.

I WAS born between Normandy and Brittany; it's called the Main. It's very agricultural countryside. The estate stood in the middle of nowhere, not even a village nearby.

I had a free childhood, a huge territory in which to play, with horses, animals, and so on. That was a good preparation to be at ease with the environment.

I suppose that if you are born in a city your body is not trained in the same way.

At a very early age, as early as I can remember, I began to paint. To paint, not to draw like a child, but seriously. I was interested in van Gogh, Cézanne, Modigliani, Gauguin, which is strange, because we were living in the middle of nowhere with no information about the art world. But I suppose if he is interested in something, a child finds his way to get information, and so I did. But I didn't study in that direction at all, because I come from a very conservative family and there was no place to be an artist there. You were expected to be a banker or diplomat or an officer or something like that.

But as soon as I found myself independent, I went back to it, to paint, and I started to make documentary films.

I WAS not looking, I was peering.

I was trying to understand the world through my eyes. I was born intensely visual.

It's strange how you can see that quality in a person.

Have you ever seen photos of Picasso? His eyes are those of an eagle.

There is a famous photo of him—I used to travel always with it. Now I've lost it—just a portrait of him, maybe by Henri Cartier-Bresson.

The gaze of Picasso is unbelievable, he is like a pirate, he wants to steal everything with his eyes.

A visual scavenger.

One day I overheard a conversation between my girlfriend and somebody else.

She said, It's a pity I didn't meet him when he had his eyes.

And I heard the other person answer, Don't regret it. He had the eyes of a murderer.

I thought it was very interesting because there is something true in it.

I really looked at things so intensely that it was a bit disturbing.

I also remember being in a café in New York when somebody stopped, looked at me, and said, Are you a painter?

And I said, Why?

He said, The way you look at things.

AFTER A certain length of time, absolute darkness becomes unbearable. I went to Greenland. I went there, maybe like Bali, to confront myself with a visually violent landscape, to force my brain to see. Well, in the north, the extreme north, most of the time it's totally dark. Month after month it is pitch dark and the very few people who live there become completely crazy.

It's too extreme.

If you put yourself in an extreme condition, like blindness, you reach something inside of you, which otherwise you wouldn't have any contact with. In that encounter you can be defeated or victorious.

Indeed, New York is really hectic, with a lot of stress of human hardship and so on. But when you go to Greenland, an island bigger than half of Europe with fifty thousand people, that's all, and with a few musk bulls, a lot of seals, some polar bears, and months of darkness, those extreme conditions give birth to a person very different from the typical New Yorker. You are so busy trying to survive that there should be no place for mental depression. And yet, in the north, the extreme north, in that long pitch-dark night, you may still become depressed, even demented. Very few people can take all that darkness.

In those extreme conditions, you are confronted with another way of life. If you are strong enough, it will free you. Of course, for that freedom you pay a high price, which is to live in the most hostile place in the world. But space, the inner space, is absolute. And then you reach something, which is the essence of yourself.

I stayed in a place called Ilulissat, a fishing village on the huge Disco Bay. Every day I went out on the banks of a fjord. That fjord is twenty-five miles long and four miles wide and in front of you pass icebergs—millions of them—as big as buildings in New York. Say you are on the bank of that fjord, totally alone, in silence, and you have Manhattan in ice passing you and floating away, disappearing to the horizon. Of course I didn't see it, but the image is so strong that it is very difficult for me to believe that I did not. It makes an enormous noise because they fall over, an explosion like an atomic bomb, and sometimes it makes a wave sixty-five feet high so you can see and hear all those skyscrapers shaking together. Did I see it?

On the bank of the fjord of Ilulissat I created my own vision.

MY LAST painting is like a premonition.

It is not finished; I was working on it when I was attacked.

It's a large picture representing a black man seen from the waist up leading a horse, of which only the head and chest are visible, and his other hand is in the hair of a young girl. Originally, the subject had been entirely different. The picture was supposed to represent a rich woman in a fur coat holding with one hand her race-horse and with the other her little daughter; in short, an illustration of selfishness, power, and money. To my great amazement, a black man with a naked, muscular torso appeared instead of this woman. Quite quickly, the picture was nearly finished, except for one detail. I found it impossible to paint the eyes of either the man or the animal; or rather, more precisely, I painted them and the canvas immediately lost all meaning.

The more I looked at it, the more aware I was of

having created, in some way, a self-portrait. Inside you is a wild horse, a little girl (Alice in Wonderland), and a very masculine character, and you are the combination of those three beings.

Finally, I left the canvas white where the horse's eyes belonged, and I rubbed the man's eyes lightly with a tissue, which had the effect of covering the sockets with skin, as if the eyelids were joined together as mine are today.

I remember I had difficulties painting the black guy because I had no model, so with a girlfriend of mine I went to Forty-second Street to a porno shop to find a torso of black guy, a powerful torso. And we were looking through all those pornographic magazines, seeing the most shocking things and laughing. And the people—you know those men, they sneak into those pornographic shops and they feel a little bit guilty—and we were not feeling guilty at all, just in need of a good model, that's all, and those people were very upset by our behavior. Looking at those things and laughing loudly about it is not the way you're supposed to act on Forty-second Street. You have to be guilty, I suppose, or at least a little bit furtive.

I WAS in Vietnam. A freelance war reporter. It was nearly the end, 1973. It was terrible, but I didn't focus on the war itself. I did focus a lot on the local population, mainly the children, and among the children mainly the orphans.

I was interested in the people who were innocent and still had to endure the consequences of such madness.

I remember arriving in an orphanage in Saigon and there were something like a thousand children in a courtyard playing wildly and in a corner was a little girl—a very, very beautiful little girl around twelve years old, looking ashamed, not playing, because she no longer had arms.

A mine had blown them up.

Those visions are still very vivid in my mind.

. . .

When I found myself in St. Vincent's hospital in New York, one of the doctors said, It is very strange you don't look so upset with this blindness.

And I said, I saw a lot.

If I had become what I was intended to be, like a worker in an office in a bank or something of the kind, probably I would have been desperate, because I would have had regrets. You know, you work in an office and you say, One day I will go to see the world. Instead, I went to see the world and I said, Maybe one day I will be obliged to work in an office.

I saw wild islands, women with gold teeth and sexes like sea anemones. I saw a white-hot island where lepers eat sharks. I saw dark islands hiding in the night, imprisoned in their own magic. Only the wind swept me along, for I had no wish to see nature in the raw, crude savagery, man without hope, whitened bones in the lagoons, children wasting away, the thousand-rupee girl, the rotting shark gazing at the leper, and all the wrecks of our gutted dreams in the cove of no return.

Yes, I saw the world.

At the end of every day Abdul Jemal, the captain of that dilapidated boat, would thrust his fist toward a hazy line of white coast on the horizon and cry, Makassar, before ordering the maneuver that would take us away on a new tack. His voice, when he pronounced the name Makassar, *took on an intonation that contained the whole city, the bars, the brothels, the stabbings, the boats arriving from every corner of that liquid country, that floating nation, those fourteen thousand islands spread between the archipelago of Java, Borneo, the Celebes, and the Philippines.*

Abdul Jemal says: "When your life depends on the wind, a great calmness descends within you."

I SAW the world very well, and in fact, I still do so. I still look at the world. Its perception is different, but it's still visual for me.

At times I am afraid that the memory I have of the visible world will disappear little by little, to be replaced by an abstract universe of sound, smell, and touch.

I force myself to visualize this hospital bedroom with its metal furniture, its window, the curtains. I bring to mind paintings, Rembrandt's Polish cavalier, Francis Bacon's portraits of Innocent X.

My ability to create images absolutely must not atrophy. I must remain capable of bringing back the world I looked at intensely for thirty-five years. By contemplating in my memory the volcano of Lombok or the perfect harmony of a building designed by Michelangelo, I continue to receive instruction and knowledge from them. That is the immense privilege of blind people who were formerly able to see.

IN ST. Vincent's hospital in New York, when I started to walk out of my room or was in the room by myself, I banged my head several times, and I was always afraid something would stick into my eyes. I wanted a form of protection, but not made of glass, because I was afraid of getting broken pieces in my eyes. So on a piece of cardboard I designed these glasses, or the mask, or whatever you want to call it.

So I now wear a band in the shape of glasses cut out of a sheet of steel. The metal reflects the lights of the city, other people's eyes, as mirrors were used to catch larks. It covers my fear, my wound, with a kind of brutal arrogance. This band rules out pity.

I knew a little Italian jeweler in SoHo and he understood what I wanted and he made it. And I must say, it does work very well for me, gives me confidence. I mean: scars, they are very private.

I HAD to learn to be helped.

I had to learn order—I was not a very ordered person—because otherwise I could not find things around in my own room, and that was quite a new way too. Patience, patience most of all, patience and acceptance. To accept being helped is probably the hardest thing.

The first time I walked out of my bedroom in the hospital, just to go to the corridor, I found myself holding the arm of a friend, and I understood: you will need help all the time and you will have to accept it.

If you are very independent and not very patient, circumstances like mine are a good school to transform your character. So I learned that as hard as I tried to be independent, still I would need help if I wanted something.

I know it's going to be difficult, but I will go at it. I will take the time needed and will go at it.

Spring has come and I feel claustrophobic, hemmed in by the city. Meanwhile, I have fallen in love with a whimsical and unpredictable ballerina. In fact, she is so unpredictable that by the end of June she has vanished in an ultimate pirouette. That is how I find myself embarking on a most extraordinary and unexpected journey.

Someone told me that she has gone to India, to the Himalayas, Kashmir, and Ladakh.

Ladakh. I try to remember. Years ago I had seen some photographs of a fertile valley amid a fantastic wilderness of stone and beyond, towering above, the far snowcapped peaks of the mountains.

I had always been reticent about going to India. I felt that I was too ignorant.

But now I am in love with this woman and I want to find her.

I STARTED to travel alone in Kashmir, then Ladakh, then Zanskar, which are valleys in the Himalayas.

I traveled alone for two months.

Nothing bad happened to me, absolutely nothing. Quite the contrary. And I think there is a good lesson in it: If you find a way to dance with people, to dance with life, nothing bad can happen to you.

I have to hope so.

I have to believe in it.

When I arrived in India—in New Delhi—at once my bag, my money, everything disappeared.

And I said, well, I have been robbed, the only thing I can do is take the next plane back to New York.

In fact, after one hour everything was brought back by those people.

They didn't say a word to me.

In silence they took my hand and they dragged me through customs and so on and gave me my money back, with some of it changed into rupees.

They put me in a three-wheeled taxi, one of those inexpensive ones.

And when I wanted to thank them and to give them a little bit of money, I couldn't find them with my hand. So I asked the driver of the taxi, "But where are they? Who are they?"

And he said, "Oh! Just beggars."

They were beggars living in the airport.

They saw me and saw I was helpless.

And they just took it on themselves to do everything for me.

And I thought, this is going to be an interesting trip.

The Imperial Hotel is an old-fashioned building on Jan-path with vast rooms. At 6:00 AM, after a short night, I start looking for the swimming pool. A very old man in a very clean loincloth and turban, with measured move-ments and a vaporous voice, leads me from the changing room to the deserted pool.

I dive in. The water is still cold from the night. I swim enthusiastically, tearing twenty hours of flight from my muscles. Suddenly something hits my forehead. For a fraction of a second, I think I am going to smash into the wall. I extend my hand and find no obstacle. I start swim-ming again, gently at first, but as I regain self-confidence, throwing myself into it once more, I am again forced to stop. A hard object had actually brushed against my nose. This time I am faster, and in one fell swoop, as if catching a fly, I grab hold of . . . my cane! Yes, my cane, just as the old man's voice directs my attention from the edge of the pool, "This way, sir, this way!"

He had noticed how I guide myself following my cane. Since it was obvious that I could not use it while swimming, he was running around the pool, pointing it in front of my nose to indicate the line I should follow. Rescued by beggars, led while swimming by a galloping grandfather—I am enchanted by such irrationality. I may not run into any serious difficulty in India after all.

IF I THINK of it, I met the most amazing people: a merchant of apricots or a monk or an errant philosopher. . . . I had no idea where we were going; I was just walking with them.

One of them, Kemala, insisted on taking me to a holy man.

The room is dark, windowless. The holy man speaks. His voice is gentle but firm. Didn't Kemala say he was a hundred and thirty years old? I would have said he was a hundred years younger. Kemala launches into a long-winded monologue, interrupted by the short, precise questions of the saint, then turns to me and says with disapproval in his voice, "He can do nothing for your eyes."

"Tell him I know, not to worry. Ask him about the young lady I'm looking for."

The holy man laughs. He asks that I sit on the mat near him. He takes my hand. I am facing him. The tips of our knees are touching. He has placed one of my hands, the right one, on his knee. Under the cotton, his skin feels surprisingly young, elastic. He seems to be enjoying our meeting. I am conscious of this by the smile in his voice, the way he puts his hand on mine, flat on his knee.

He says, "Learn to live slowly. That way there will be no hazard in death." Kemala translates.

As I prepare to leave him, I almost feel as though I am abandoning him to his strange destiny, sitting there on his cushion in this dark room.

Suddenly, he grabs hold of my hand again just as I am getting up and says, "Surviving life is everything." I find the idea hilarious, and we laugh heartily together.

I SPENT two months in those Himalayan valleys, walking with all those people. From those narrow valleys, land begins its ascent toward the surrounding monstrosity; its mass does not seem to grow out of the earth but to descend from the sky.

At night, between the infinite and myself, I can hear an imperceptible whistling—God whistling between his teeth, the sharp iced peaks.

Suddenly beauty stabs me like a dagger. The pain of perceiving beauty without seeing it!

Today it's impossible for me to think that I didn't see it.

My brain fabricated such strong images, they are so vividly printed there.

Just the touch of the air on your skin reveals to you the luminosity of the sky.

There was a young girl; she was born blind. One day

her mother saw her climbing in a tree. She ran to save her daughter: "What do you think you are doing?"

"I'm trying to touch the blue of the sky," said the little girl.

Well, in the Himalayas, I did touch the blue of the sky.

My bag is not meant for trekking. I keep shifting it from shoulder to shoulder, but after a while both shoulders hurt just as much. I try to relieve the pain by carrying it on my head, but the load only makes my body stiff, forcing me to walk like a robot. We are heading toward a monastery where Krishna, a merchant, wants to buy the apricot harvest. We have been walking for some time, and the path is very steep. Suddenly, the characteristic hammering of little hooves on the ground. A donkey!

Jullays! Jullays! Greetings! I try to explain to the owner that I want to rent it.

Everyone laughs, but no one understands. Finally the man begins to suspect a change in the course of his journey when I take hold of the donkey's halter, forcing the animal to make a half-turn, placing its tail where its head had been a few seconds before. Next, I poise my bag on its withers; sit astride the tiny mount, and, pointing up ahead, cry "Gompa!"—Monastery!—as you would cry

"Charge!" There is a moment's silence, then they burst out laughing. The owner agrees to twenty rupees, but the donkey has not been consulted. With all the obstinacy of its breed, it refuses to budge an inch. Krishna tries to push the animal, then remembers a universal technique and grabs hold of its tail, twisting it violently. It takes off with a bolt, to its own surprise.

Sometimes I sleep on the ground, right on the track.

All is quiet. The silence is awesome. Lying under the stars, cradled in the warmth of my blanket, I drift off into the temptation of the invisible.

I DON'T like to travel. I mean, when I travel I don't like to move. I can sit on a stone and listen to what's going on. I can stay weeks and weeks without doing anything other than just concentrating on understanding and making connections with people there.

One has to learn to move less, to travel vertically and to go more and more into harmony, silence, and beauty.

Finally the ground levels out. We enter a little circus-shaped valley. "Gompa," says one of the monks, taking my hand and pointing it up. Between the peaks the great monastery of Rizong stands in all its majesty.

As we reach the top of the steps, the monks gather around me. Among them I notice the voices of very young boys, children, little novices no doubt. They laugh and blurt out high-pitched interjections. Yet despite their constant energy, a sense of peace emanates from their brouhaha. They guide me to a terrace where I am presented to the rimpoche, the abbot. He takes the fingers of my left hand in his hand; although I understand not a word of what he is saying, my fingers perceive that I am welcome. Beside him, a monk translates into somewhat tantric English. The rimpoche says, "Come under our roof and stay as long as you wish. The food is very bad. Why did you come?"

. . .

After a few days, the monks seem to have totally adopted me in a unique way and let me sleep on a high terrace. Lama Lampu, the translator, calls it the Terrace of Solitude.

In the morning I hear sandals shuffling. "Jullay! Jullay!" It is Lama Lampu. He sits down. The cry of a bird of prey tears through the air, and way down in the valley, lost among the trees, I can hear water flowing. Lama Lampu touches my chest and laughs. He says that my insistence on sleeping in the open air leaves me vulnerable to all kinds of spirits who willingly enter into me. He says that my face is still dark from the night. We get up and go to breakfast on some miserable concoction.

The kitchen, buzzing with activity, is a square room with a high ceiling. In the middle a charcoal fire is kept burning all day long. The room is full of smoke; the vault, walls, shelves, all seem cooked; everything is black with soot except for the shiny brass and copper utensils. The smoke floats in the room without seeming to bother the monks, who melt into the monochrome background. Framed by the small openings pierced in the thick wall, the landscape seems all the brighter. We sit down by a window with our small wooden bowls.

Lama Lampu guides me everywhere, makes me touch everything, see everything. The great façade, with its classical, uncluttered, serene layout, hides an extraordinary labyrinth of corridors, passages, split levels, corners, and terraces jutting out under the sky. The original chaos, disorder of the soul, ferreting through thought. Unexpected passages, windows looking out onto walls, rooms apparently without purpose. But after a while, one realizes that all this imbroglio of architecture corresponds to well-determined functions, that there is reason in the madness.

In the main sanctuary he stands on my left, his right arm around my waist, and takes my right hand, not only to direct me but to apply it to books centuries old, to the chair reserved for the Dalai Lama, to the multiple statues of the incarnations of Buddha. He spares me nothing. And, of course, according to the rules, we walk around the sanctuary clockwise. A sequence from the film Some Like It Hot springs to my mind, and I close my hand over Lama Lampu's and draw him into a tango, keeping the beat with onomatopoeia. "Ta-DUM, ta-DUM, tadada-DUM." There is no question that this is the first tango ever danced in a Himalayan monastery. The monks guffaw, and my behavior, which surprises even me, does not seem to shock them at all.

I NEVER found the ballerina, but I did find my old freedom again—and, you might say, even more.

ONE DAY a friend of mine said, How do you imagine my face?

I said, What do you mean? I knew you before I lost my sight!

And he said, No, you didn't.

I said, But think, I swear I saw you.

He said, No you never saw me.

And I thought, Is he right?

So we calculated and he was right. But I know exactly how he looks.

Yet I don't know if he looks like that.

Vision is a creation.

It's not just perception.

I experiment with it all the time.

When I walk in the street with somebody, I'll ask the person, what is there? Many people say: A wall, or they say, a tree. But they don't see anything.

If I walk with a friend of mine who is a painter, who has the most acute eye I know, to walk with him in the street is a trip. I mean it's an adventure because he sees.

He creates a vision, and he gives it to me.

. . .

I think there is no reality in fact. What you see would be different from what your neighbor sees, so who has the reality?

Again: Vision is a creation.

That's why some people see and some people don't see.

Much the way they hear music or they hear noise.

I think people are like that with their eyes. They are not interested by what they see and they don't really understand it.

They use vision not to bump into a tree or fall into a ditch.

This painter friend of mine, he said to paint is to see beyond.

I think this is true not only of painting.

To see is always to see beyond. To stand behind the appearance. There is a world behind the exact world.

I want to convince people that the eyes of their soul can also see.

TO SEE, one should liberate oneself from the immediate. Looking beyond opens the world to where beauty has become one with truth. The harmony of the invisible is always more beautiful than the one of the visible.

I was talking with a Scandinavian architect about the icebergs in Greenland and he told me that for many years when he was young he had pictures of icebergs in his bedroom, and they became an important inspiration for his architecture. You know, it is very interesting, he saw something that nobody else saw, which was the architecture in an iceberg.

　　With sounds it's the same thing. Do you know Olivier Messiaen, the composer? Almost everyone has heard the sound of birds, but he created a musical world with what he heard in the sounds of birds. Since human ears existed, nobody else ever heard what his soul created through his ear.

. . .

One day, the only thing I heard of Glenn Gould playing Bach were the creaks of his chair and his humming. I like that. Some people are disturbed by it; I'm not at all. I think it's extremely moving to listen to his inner music. It is not Bach; it is Glenn Gould. Even the creaking of his chair shows emotion.

Even with good ears and good eyes, you can be deaf to music and blind to beauty. I mean, unable to create with your ears or your eyes.

After losing my sight, I discovered that in fact I had listened very little to music and even to people. I was too busy looking.

I loved music but I was not *into* music. I was too busy with my eyes.

After losing them, I started to get passionate about music.

So when I went to that rehabilitation center, I said I wanted to learn to play the piano.

And so I started lessons, but they were teaching it in a very boring way with Braille, so you always had to have one hand on the score. How can you play piano with one hand?

I heard of this young Russian professor in New

York and, with him, I really started to play piano at age thirty-five.

It released my soul.

Much better to play the piano than to take Valium.

WHAT IS vision exactly?

In the book I wrote in Bali, I talked a little bit about it, but not so much about the process. I just described very precisely what I see—inner landscapes—without giving much explanation. So the editor would write all the time in the margins of the manuscript: "How do you know?" How do I know? That was exactly the purpose of the book!

Blindness is a drastic face-to-face with yourself. It forces you to look inside yourself, and if it is dark you see nothing. My vision is based on inner landscapes. Many people don't see their inner landscapes because they don't look inside. They think, since it's inside, it must be dark, so there is nothing to see.

I wrote about a trip I took to the Himalayas and described very precisely what I saw—which I didn't see at all—my visions.

My travel is entirely imaginary, that's where its strength lies.

. . .

My book was read by a professor, a researcher in perception. He was very interested in the process of the brain in creating vision.

Professor Richard L. Gregory of the Perceptual Systems Research Centre at the Department of Psychology of the University of Bristol studied a man who had lost his sight at the age of ten months and was given back his sight when he was fifty-three. Still, after the operation, he could perceive images, but he could see nothing. Or rather, he couldn't understand what he was perceiving.

Vision is more than just eye function. A camera perceives, it doesn't see. Blindness has long-term effects on how the brain processes information and constructs one's view of the world.

You could say, a blind person who sees becomes blind.

He has perception, he is confused, he doesn't have vision.

Once I asked a born-blind teenager, If tomorrow sight could be given to you with a simple surgery, what would be your decision?

He kept silent for a while and then said, I would be afraid images would suppress my imagination.

Isn't it what is happening to most of us in this new world of the visually obese?

Dr. Gregory's patient, when they removed the bandage from over his eyes—he saw something moving toward his bed and a hole opening in it and the voice of his wife coming out of that hole, so he thought, Eh! That must be my wife. And he divorced her. In his case, the image destroyed the imaginary.

Not only didn't he like what he was seeing but he didn't understand it.

I also asked that born-blind teenager, Can you imagine the sea?

He answered, Not completely. I can imagine the waves, but the waste of water toward the infinite, that is difficult. Infinity is hard to figure out, especially when it ends not so far away, on the horizon. It's easier to imagine what you can hold in your hands, in your arms, but beyond . . .

Professor Gregory's patient certainly could hold his wife in his arms, and yet . . .

TYPICAL MALE reaction: blindness is equivalent to castration.

At the beginning I couldn't believe it, but it is very much like that in their minds.

Even in the Bible you can find something of the sort with the marvelous story of Samson. If you read the story you will see what happens to him, that being blinded is a kind of castration.

And Oedipus, having slept with his mother and engendered children from the womb he came from and so on, the first thing he does is not to cut off his balls, it's to pierce his eyes.

In the male, brain blindness and castration are linked.

I knew a man who was madly jealous of his wife, berserk with jealousy, but he would never think anything of my staying alone with his wife in the same room or sleeping in the house, even with him not there.

Because no—from there, there is no danger.

I thought that was quite extraordinary.

I could see how jealous he was of anybody else, and with me he was completely at ease.

YES, I have regrets.

I would prefer to see—definitely—and if tomorrow somebody tells me about the possibility, I will jump on it.

I think it has made my life much more complicated.

But I also try to use it as a yoga.

Yet I don't succeed all the time.

Sometimes I get very exhausted.

When you are exhausted and you cannot reach what you want, you become depressed.

And then you have to be careful.

Clear your mind of all negative thinking, it's too dangerous.

Since I lost my sight I have had two very close friends commit suicide, and they told me they couldn't understand why I didn't commit suicide.

Suicide? No. Orders are to go on living, meanly, painfully, scrupulously.

. . .

One of my friends was a heroin junkie.

He died four years ago of an overdose at age fifty-three.

A great painter, a great artist—very successful, with a beautiful wife and daughter.

He couldn't understand why I wasn't taking heroin.

I remember Rothko's work very well. Before the black period that came at the end, he did paintings that were complete magnifications of light and silence. They are the most spiritual visions (whatever you may mean by that word, *spiritual;* a very difficult word to use).

The chapel he did in Houston is so enlightening. You don't know why, but you are in a temple, a spiritual machine. Well, look what happened to Rothko. He drank himself to death. When he started the black paintings he was practically in a delirium. A very good friend of his said to me then, It's terrible he is killing himself.

Why was he drinking? I have no answer.

Why do people destroy themselves, why do people commit suicide? Why, during or after what I went through, did I never contemplate suicide?

I have no answers.

I have the feeling that the only sin is the sin of Judas, the one who sold Jesus Christ for thirty pieces of silver or whatever, and went into despair and hanged himself.

Such is the absolute sin. The sin against life.

NIGHTS CRUMBLE.

What is obvious is that the adventure that creates freedom and provides answers can no longer be pursued in the same way. And in any case, in order to go further, I definitely had to change. Adventure is revolt, not to be resigned, the opposite of cynicism.

By adventure I mean everything that is opposed to the loss of consideration for life. No injury is irreparable but death.

If you have a clear vision of the human condition, a bit of a brain, and a certain distance from yourself, really nothing is tragic—but the Human Condition itself.

What is happening to me is happening to all of humanity.

And what is happening in the wars, in the prisons, in the torture chambers of the world is happening to me as an individual.

Revenge? Pardon? In a strange way it doesn't concern me. All I know is that if I seek revenge, if I dwell into hate, I will find myself trapped in the past, obsessed by what they have done to me, unable to project myself into the future. So, on top of having destroyed my eyes, they would have imputed my life from its future, killed my life. I have no time for them.

To attain one's dimension is the very goal of the adventure. To satisfy your Destiny. To become One.

Whatever we do, there is always hope for redemption.

If I lose hope, then I will commit suicide.

Do you know the writings of Primo Levi? At Auschwitz, he was put in a situation where to live was impossible, yet through a formidable instinct and strength of character and fight, he survived. Very few survived. And yet, many years later, he committed suicide. Why? He knew something that he didn't write about; he came out from that death camp without God and without Man.

He knew that you can live without God, but you can't live without Man—that is to say, without believing in Man.

Why do you want to live, why do you want to die?

. . .

I think as long as you wake up in the morning full of hope, you are in a good shape.

If you wake up in the morning and you just want to turn your back and go back to sleep, you are in great danger.

And sometimes it happens to me.

TO DESPAIR of life is to not know what life can bring you. It can bring redemption, not in a religious way, but redemption in a vital way.

Suddenly I found myself lying on a bed in a hospital thinking my life was finished. Then ten years later I found myself creating a ballet in Warsaw. I would never have thought life would turn out like this.

Many people think the loss of my sight has been a terrible rupture in my life. But no, it's not a rupture at all—life just went on, but in a different way.

There was a rupture in my physical condition, yes, but not in my destiny. It is *my* destiny.

After losing my sight, I never thought I would do something so visual as that ballet. I created a ballet, *Pas de Deux*. I wrote the story, designed the stage set, and selected the music, mixed it, and created the sound track. And that ballet was danced at the Grand Opera of Warsaw. For me it was quite extraordinary to do a show, a visual show. And when I did it, I didn't think, It is a challenge. No. I just did it for this friend of mine who is a ballet dancer, a brilliant one, so she is invited to international festivals to dance anything she chooses.

So I said, You do the choreography, and I'll do the "argument," as it is called in French, that is to say the theme, just for fun. I didn't do it to prove anything, but just because it was so exciting.

After I wrote the "theme," I designed the décor, which was inspired by a Hopper painting called *Hotel by a Railroad*. Well, I needed somebody just sitting at a bar onstage, an extra. I couldn't find anybody, so finally I put myself onstage, which was quite overwhelming. Me in front of that monster, the audience. I couldn't see it, but I could feel its breath—so very strong! It's looking at you with thousand eyes and you are looking at it with your soul.

Strangely enough, I must say blindness didn't change my life that much.

I thought it would drastically change, but I must observe that it has not.

It made me more forceful in obtaining what I want.

WHAT WE are all looking for is the sense of life.

And the sense of life *is* life.

Once you have understood that, you can relax.

The sense of life is not to go to the realms of God and all that.

Eternity is now.

There is no future. The future is now.

The sense of life *is* life.

If you talk with quantum physicists they will tell you about the Wall of Planck, which occurred 10^{-43} of a second after the Big Bang (or the supposed Big Bang). We don't know exactly.

Behind that wall, not only space, but time disappears.

You cannot imagine a universe without space, where there is no more time.

It's impossible for your brain to grasp it.

But it means something.

That probably time doesn't exist.

That eternity is now.

At the end you must know that you will be defeated.

You will be defeated by age. Age is an enemy against which you can do nothing.

Because to be old is not easy, but to be old and blind, that's very tiring.

You better eat life while you can because at the end, like everybody else, your body will be defeated.

At least your mind can be triumphant, independent.

THE FACT that I lost my sight is very spectacular, but there are things which are much more terrible.

The other day I took a taxi.

The driver was a little Cambodian guy, and in a very nice way he said, What happened to you? Is it that you are just sick but your vision will come back, no?

And I said, For the moment, it's permanent.

And he said, Oh I cannot express my emotion toward what happened to you.

I said, That is very kind of you, but you know, it's very nice because of course you can see what happened to me and you give me your compassion, but you know there are so many people much more wounded than me, and you see nothing and they don't receive any compassion.

And the guy was silent for a moment, then he said, Monsieur, I understand very well what you say because my wife and my four children were killed in front of me in Cambodia.

. . .

So there he was, driving his cab in Paris with this huge wound that nobody could see.

It's not comparable.

That is much worse.

WHY DO I travel?
  Why do I go to see places?
  I don't know.
  But I hope one day I will get tired of it.

ACKNOWLEDGMENTS

Thanks . . .

to Laure de Gramont without whom this book would not have existed.

to Judith Curr who invented this book.

to Peter Borland who has been the most patient and enthusiastic editor.

and to everyone who held out their hand to me on the path to light.

ABOUT THE AUTHOR

HUGUES DE MONTALEMBERT, a French painter and photographer, was blinded during a violent assault while living in New York in 1978. His story was also the basis of the acclaimed documentary film *Black Sun*. He currently lives in Paris.